D0590432

Welcome to the Disney Learning Programme!

Sharing a book with your children is the perfect opportunity to cuddle and enjoy the reading experience together. Research has shown that reading aloud to and with your children is one of the most important ways to prepare them for success as a reader. When you share books with each other, you help strengthen your children's reading and vocabulary skills as well as stimulate their curiosity, imagination and enthusiasm for reading.

Dory, a blue fish, lives with Marlin and his son Nemo on the Great Barrier Reef. Dory suffers from short-term memory loss, but one day she remembers that she has a family. She thinks her family is in California – a long way from the reef! She sets off on a journey to find her parents. By chance, Dory is caught in a net and ends up in the Marine Life Institute. She makes many friends who try to help her find her parents. She has to be brave and resourceful, but in the end it is friendship that saves the day!

You can help your children enjoy the story even more by talking to them about how family and friends help each other. Perhaps you have a story about missing your family when you were a child! Children find it easier to understand what they read when they can connect it with their own personal experiences.

Children learn in different ways and at different speeds, but they all require a supportive environment to nurture a lifelong love of books, reading and learning. The Adventures in Reading books are carefully levelled to present new challenges to developing readers. They are filled with familiar and fun characters from the wonderful world of Disney to make the learning experience comfortable, positive and enjoyable.

Enjoy your reading adventure together!

Scholastic Children's Books,
Euston House,
24 Eversholt Street,
London NW1 1DB, UK

A division of Scholastic Ltd
London • New York • Toronto • Sydney • Auckland
Mexico City • New Delhi • Hong Kong

This book was first published in the United States in 2016
by Random House Children's Books, a division of Penguin Random House LLC.
This edition published in the UK by Scholastic Ltd, 2016.

ISBN 978 14071 6582 0

Printed in Malaysia

2 4 6 8 10 9 7 5 3 1

Papers used by Scholastic Children's Books are made from woods grown in sustainable forests.

www.scholastic.co.uk

Ocean Adventure

By Bill Scollon
Illustrated by
the Disney Storybook Art Team

Dory is a blue fish.
She lives on a coral reef in the ocean.
Her friends Marlin and Nemo live
there, too.

Once, Nemo got lost.
Dory helped Marlin find Nemo.
They all came home to the reef.

Dory is happy on the reef.
But one day she remembers her
mum and dad.
They were blue fish too.

Dory remembers something else …
Her parents are in California.
California is a long way away!

Dory leaves the coral reef.
She swims into the deep,
dark ocean.
She wants to find her mum
and dad.

Marlin and Nemo want to help her.
They can help her get to California.

Dory is caught and put in a tank.
Hank is a red octopus. He tells
Dory she is in the Marine Life
Institute.

Dory remembers that name!
Her mum and dad are here.

Hank wants to help Dory find her
mum and dad.
He helps her to
meet Bailey.

Bailey helps Dory to meet Destiny!
Destiny remembers Dory.
She knows where Dory's mum
and dad are.

Destiny says Dory must get to the
Open Ocean exhibit.
Dory meets a cute brown otter.
He wants to help Dory.

Marlin and Nemo need to find Dory.
Becky the loon helps them.

Dory meets Hank again.
They hide in the touch pool.

Soon they make it to the Open
Ocean exhibit. Dory is happy.
She will see her mum and dad.

Dory sees pink coral.
It is just like her home on the reef.
She is excited.

Will she see her mum and dad?
She can't wait.

Dory sees some yellow fish.
She does not see her mum and dad.
She feels so sad.

She swims through green kelp.
She does not know what to do.

Dory sees a path of white shells.
Dory follows the path.

Two blue fish dash out.
It's Dory's mum and dad!

All of Dory's friends are happy.
Dory loves her colourful family and friends.

ACTIVITIES TO SHARE WITH YOUR CHILD

Now you've shared the book with your child, encourage them to try these activities with you to strengthen their understanding of the story and its themes.

FRIENDS

Dory has lots of friends. Do you know them all?
Point to the picture and say each character's name.

Marlin   Becky   Destiny

Bailey   Nemo   Hank

COLOURS

Dory and her friends are so colourful.
Look at each picture and describe the colours you can see.

HELPING EACH OTHER

Dory helped Marlin find Nemo.
Then Dory's friends helped her!
Match each picture to the right sentence.

Hank helped Dory
get out of the
touch pool.

The otter wanted
to help Dory.

Destiny told Dory
where her mum
and dad were.

Becky the loon
helped Marlin
and Nemo.

FEELINGS

Dory has a big adventure. She has to be brave, but she is happy in the end.

Look at the pictures. How do you think Dory is feeling? Use the words below to help you.

shocked   lonely   sad   happy

STORYTELLING

Use these pictures and questions to help you retell the story.

Who is Dory looking for?

Where is Dory now?

What happens in the end?

?

What else does Dory swim through?

What does Destiny tell Dory?

Where are Dory and Hank going?

Does Dory find her mum and dad in the coral?

Goodbye from Dory and friends!